MW01130579

The ALBERTOSAURUS MYSTERY

Philip Currie's Hunt in the Badlands

by T. V. Padma

Consultant: Philip J. Currie, Ph.D.
FRSC, University of Alberta

BEARPORT
PUBLISHING

New York, New York

Credits

Cover, Joseph Nettis / Photo Researchers; Title Page, Richard Nowitz; 4, Eva Koppelhus; 5, Philip Currie; 6, Richard Nowitz; 7, Richard Nowitz; 8, Neg. #19508s / American Museum of Natural History; 9, Betmann / Corbis; 10, Gail Mooney / Corbis; 11, Neg #19502s / American Museum of Natural History; 12, Neg #gsc201735a / National Resources Canada; 13, Neg #GEO85857_7c / The Field Museum, Chicago; 15, Richard Nowitz; 16, Natural History Museum Picture Library, London; 17T, © SuperStock; 17B, © Winfried Wisniewski / SuperStock; 18, Philip Currie; 19, Michael S. Yamashita / Corbis; 21, Richard Nowitz; 22, Rich Reid / Animals Animals – Earth Scenes; 23, Museum of the Rockies; 24, Carlos Goldin / Photo Researchers, Inc.; 25, Louie Psihoyos / Science Faction; 26, Richard Nowitz; 27, AP Wide World Photos; 28–29 Rodica Prato; 28, Kathrin Ayer; 29T, ticktock Media Ltd.; 29B, Joe Tucciarone.

Publisher: Kenn Goin
Editorial Director: Adam Siegel
Editorial Development: Natalie Lunis
Creative Director: Spencer Brinker
Photo Researcher: Beaura Kathy Ringrose
Design: Dawn Beard Creative

Padma thanks Adam, Ambujam, Natalie, Paul, Philip, and Rainer for support.

Library of Congress Cataloging-in-Publication Data
Padma, T. V.
   The Albertosaurus mystery : Philip Currie's hunt in the Badlands / by T.V. Padma.
      p. cm. — (Fossil hunters)
   Includes bibliographical references and index.
   ISBN-13: 978-1-59716-254-8 (lib. bdg.)
   ISBN-10: 1-59716-254-X (lib. bdg.)
   ISBN-13: 978-1-59716-282-1 (pbk.)
   ISBN-10: 1-59716-282-5 (pbk.)
   1. Albertosaurus—Alberta—Juvenile literature. 2. Currie, Philip J.—Juvenile literature.
   3. Paleontology—Cretaceous—Juvenile literature. I. Title. II. Series.

   QE862.S3P33 2007
   567.912—dc22
                              2006009950

For more information, write to Bearport Publishing Company, Inc., 101 Fifth Avenue, Suite 6R, New York, New York 10003. Printed in the United States of America.

10 9 8 7 6 5 4 3 2 1

Table of Contents

Searching Without a Map

Philip Currie was thirsty and tired. It was one of the hottest summer days of 1997. He and his team were looking for **fossils** that belonged to a dinosaur called *Albertosaurus* (al-*bur*-toh-SOR-uhss).

Philip Currie

Many fossils are buried in Canada's **badlands**. More than 40 kinds of dinosaurs once lived there.

Almost 90 years earlier, a famous fossil hunter named Barnum Brown had found a **fossil field** in western Canada's badlands. Many albertosaurs were buried in it. Philip was trying to find this place again.

It was like looking for a needle in a haystack. Brown had not made a map or written down where he had found the fossils. Philip had few **clues**—just some notes and four old photos.

The badlands of western Canada are full of hills. Philip didn't know which hill held Brown's fossils.

Discovery!

The team was running out of water. Everyone except Philip went back to the **camp**. He continued on with the search. Sand flies and mosquitoes bit him. His head hurt.

Philip had seen the remains of Brown's campsite earlier in the day. He knew the bones must be close.

Philip was trying to find the location of *Albertosaurus* fossils shown in Brown's old photograph.

All alone, Philip climbed another hill. He stopped to hold up a photo. It looked just like the scene in front of him. He also could see that years ago someone had dug into the rock there. Philip had found Brown's **bone bed**!

Holes or cuts in rocky hills are clues that someone might have dug there before.

Brown's photo was old, but Philip could see that the hills still looked the same.

Barnum the Bone Hunter

   Barnum Brown grew up in Kansas in the late 1800s. His family dug and sold coal. Young Barnum saw his first fossil when the family **plow** accidentally pulled one out of the ground.

   Brown went on to study fossils. He found that he liked digging up bones more than learning about them in class. So he left Columbia University to become a bone hunter for the American Museum of Natural History in New York City.

When fossil hunting, Brown sometimes dressed up and wore a fur coat.

Brown was very good at finding fossils. Henry Fairfield Osborn, the head of the museum, joked that Brown could "smell fossils." News writers called him "Mr. Bones."

At the American Museum of Natural History, Brown helped put together the bones he found.

When Osborn and Brown started working for the American Museum of Natural History in the 1890s, it had few dinosaur fossils. By the time Osborn died in 1935, it had more dinosaur bones than most other museums.

Finding the First *T. rex*

In the early 1900s, Brown dug up *Tyrannosaurus rex* (ti-*ran*-uh-SOR-uhss REKS) skeletons, first in Wyoming, and later in Montana. These were the first *T. rex* skeletons ever found.

In 1908, Brown found this *T. rex* skeleton. It can be seen at the American Museum of Natural History in New York City.

For several years, Brown returned to Montana to dig for fossils. The bones he found there were often stuck in hard rock. He sometimes used **dynamite** to get them out.

Then in 1910 a terrible thing happened in Brown's life. His wife died. Brown tried to forget his sadness by hunting for more fossils. He rafted down Red Deer River **Canyon** in Canada. He camped in the area, and looked for bones. Soon, Brown made a surprising discovery.

Brown (right) and his flatboat on Red Deer River

Most of the time, fossil hunters don't use dynamite because it can break fossils.

Finding Many Meat-Eaters

In Canada, Brown found a place where many skeletons were buried. The skeletons belonged to *Albertosaurus*, a large meat-eating dinosaur. It was the first time anyone had found the bones of so many meat-eating dinosaurs in the same spot.

Joseph B. Tyrrell

The first *Albertosaurus* fossils were found in 1884 by Joseph B. Tyrrell, a scientist who worked for the Canadian government.

Brown dug up some of the bones. He wrote only a few lines about his find but didn't say how unusual it was. He didn't say why he thought so many individuals of the same **species** were together. He didn't tell what this discovery might mean.

The *Albertosaurus* bones were sent to the museum and put away. There they lay in a basement storage room for many years with other dinosaur fossils.

Albertosaurus **got its name because the dinosaur's fossils were first found in Alberta, Canada.**

A Fierce Family

Albertosaurus was part of a family of **fierce**, meat-eating dinosaurs called **tyrannosaurids**. *Tyrannosaurus rex* was also part of this family.

Albertosaurus was smaller than *Tyrannosaurus rex*, but it was strong. *Albertosaurus* could see and smell well. It had many sharp teeth. Its huge, powerful jaws could crush bone.

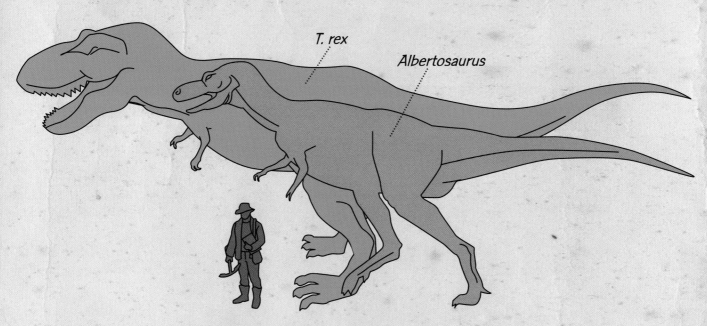

T. rex

Albertosaurus

Tyrannosaurus rex was about 40 feet (12 m) long.
Albertosaurus was about 30 feet (9 m) long.

The time of the dinosaurs lasted for about 150 million years. Tyrannosaurids lived during the last 30 million years of this time period.

Like *Tyrannosaurus rex*, *Albertosaurus* lived and hunted alone. At least, that's what **paleontologists** thought. One man was about to change their thinking, however. He had some new ideas about these **ancient** creatures.

Albertosaurus had about 70 teeth in its gigantic jaws.

Philip Currie's Questions

In 1976, Philip Currie read what Brown wrote about the **site** full of albertosaurs. At that time, most paleontologists thought tyrannosaurids lived alone. If so, asked Philip, why were many of these animals buried together? Had they died together? Had they lived together?

Some plant-eating dinosaurs had lived in groups. Maybe some of the meat-eaters that hunted them did, too, thought Philip. After all, big groups of animals were hard to hunt alone. Maybe albertosaurs hunted in **packs**.

Centrosaurus **and other plant-eating dinosaurs lived and traveled in groups.**

Philip was busy learning about many kinds of fossils and dinosaurs, however. He put his questions away for many years, just as Brown had put away his fossils.

Some animals today, such as wolves, hunt in packs. Others, such as cheetahs, usually hunt alone.

Animals must be smart to hunt as a group. Many scientists thought that tyrannosaurids and other meat-eating dinosaurs were not smart enough to hunt together.

The Bones in the Basement

Philip thought about his questions again 20 years later. This time, however, something happened that made him hunt for answers.

Philip came across some *Albertosaurus* bones in the basement of the American Museum of Natural History—the museum where Barnum Brown had worked. He could tell that the bones were from the badlands in Canada where Brown had been searching for fossils.

This fossil foot bone from an *Albertosaurus* was first discovered by Barnum Brown in Alberta, Canada, and then rediscovered by Philip Currie in New York City.

Philip saw that Brown had found at least nine albertosaurs in one spot. He also saw that Brown had taken only a few bones from each animal. More bones were still buried in the badlands, waiting to be discovered.

The American Museum of Natural History, where Brown's *Albertosaurus* **fossils were stored**

Museums often have more bones than they can put on display. They store the extra bones in rooms where students and scientists can study them.

The Bones in the Badlands

Philip discovered more than bones at the museum. He also found Brown's **field notes** and a photo of Brown's site. Using these clues, Philip was able to find the bone bed.

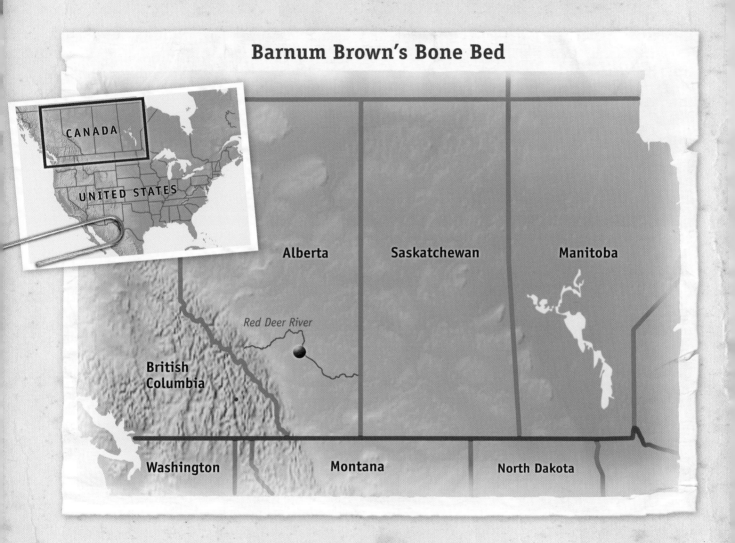

Barnum Brown's Bone Bed

CANADA

UNITED STATES

Alberta Saskatchewan Manitoba

Red Deer River

British
Columbia

Washington Montana North Dakota

● Place where Philip rediscovered
the *Albertosaurus* fossil site first
found by Barnum Brown

Locating the spot was just the first step, however. Philip and his team worked for months to dig out each fossil. At least 22 albertosaurs were buried in the rock.

After the work was done, a new question came up. Did finding many fossils together prove that the animals had lived, died, and even hunted as a group?

Philip uncovering *Albertosaurus* bones in the badlands

In the days of Barnum Brown, fossil hunters were not always able to keep good records. Today, paleontologists carefully record their finds with photographs, drawings, maps, and reports.

What May Have Happened

Philip knew there could be other reasons for the fossils being together. Many of these ideas only brought up more questions, however.

For example, the albertosaurs could have died in **quicksand**. Yet different kinds of dinosaurs could die in quicksand. Philip had found the fossils of only one kind—*Albertosaurus*.

Quicksand in Alaska

Maybe the albertosaurs had gathered to lay eggs. If so, however, the fossils should have been about the same age and size. Yet Philip had found small, young animals as well as large, old animals.

Philip's hunt had ended. Yet he needed more evidence to show that the meat-eaters had lived together.

A reconstructed nest of fossilized dinosaur eggs

Scientists know that dinosaurs laid eggs because fossil eggs of several kinds of dinosaurs have been found.

More Groups of Meat-Eaters

More evidence came when a paleontologist named Rodolfo Coria phoned Philip. Coria was calling from Argentina. He also had found a spot where a group of meat-eating dinosaurs was buried. So perhaps meat-eaters did live in groups after all.

Rodolfo Coria uncovers teeth on a huge dinosaur jawbone.

Scientists found more places with groups of meat-eating dinosaurs. These places were all over—Arizona, Montana, South Dakota, Utah, Mongolia, and Zimbabwe.

Philip also looked carefully at the footprints of meat-eating dinosaurs in the Peace River Canyon of Canada. The footprints showed that meat-eating dinosaurs may have traveled together.

In 1966 and 1976, paleontologists found footprints of groups of meat-eating dinosaurs in Australia and in the Connecticut River Valley in the United States.

Philip Currie investigating dinosaur footprints in Alberta, Canada

Digging Deeper

Did some meat-eating dinosaurs spend time living and hunting together? Scientists still aren't sure. They can only make smart guesses based on the fossils they have found.

Other questions are still unanswered as well. Why did the albertosaurs at Brown's site die? What killed so many animals at one time? A big storm? A forest fire?

By studying fossils, experts can create models like this life-size *Albertosaurus.*

Philip Currie says that a paleontologist is like a detective. The mysterious death happened millions of years ago. No one saw it. Using clues, the scientist tries to tell what happened, how, and why. As long as there are fossils waiting to be found, the investigation continues.

Philip Currie and many other paleontologists are now looking into the question of whether birds are the **descendants** of meat-eating dinosaurs.

Philip is holding up the fossil of a dinosaur that had feathers. The feathers were probably used to keep the animal warm, not to fly.

A Trip Back in Time: Who Lived with *Albertosaurus*?

Dinosaurs lived on Earth for around 150 million years. Scientists divide the time in which the dinosaurs lived into three periods—the Triassic period (250 to 205 million years ago), the Jurassic period (205 to 145 million years ago), and the Cretaceous period (145 to 65 million years ago).

Albertosaurus lived from about 71 to 68 million years ago, during the Cretaceous period. Here are three prehistoric animals that lived at the same time as *Albertosaurus*.

Hypacrosaurus

Hypacrosaurus was first found by Barnum Brown in Alberta, Canada. These plant-eating dinosaurs may have been eaten by *Albertosaurus*.

FACTS

Hypacrosaurus
(hye-*pak*-ruh-SOR-uhss)

- has a name that means "very high lizard"
- had a mouth shaped like a duck's bill and a body part called a *crest* on top of its head
- probably came together in groups for at least part of the year
- had a call that may have sounded like a deep trumpet
- **size:** about 30 feet (9 m) long

Daspletosaurus

Like *Albertosaurus* and *T. rex*, this meat-eating dinosaur was a member of the tyrannosaurid family. It was probably more powerful than *Albertosaurus* but less powerful than *T. rex*.

FACTS

Daspletosaurus
(dass-*plee*-toh-SOR-uhss)

- has a name that means "frightful lizard"
- had a head almost as large as the head of a *Tyrannosaurus rex* and teeth the size of bananas
- probably ate mostly horned dinosaurs
- **size:** about 28 feet (8.5 m) long

Quetzalcoatlus

This creature looked like a giant pelican and may have flown in the sky above albertosaurs. Not a dinosaur, it belonged to the animal group called pterosaurs (TERR-uh-*sorz*). Pterosaurs were flying reptiles.

FACTS

Quetzalcoatlus
(kwet-zal-koh-AHT-lus)

- named after one of the gods of the Aztecs, a people who built a great civilization in Mexico during the 1400s and 1500s
- may have eaten by gliding over the water and scooping up fish in its beak
- **size:** had a 40-foot (12-m) wingspan and was about the size of a small plane

Glossary

ancient (AYN-shunt)
very old

badlands (BAD-landz)
an area with rocks that have
been sculpted into unusual
shapes by harsh winds and rain

bone bed (BOHN BED)
a place where many fossils are
found

camp (KAMP)
a place outdoors where people
stay for a short time

canyon (KAN-yuhn)
a steep-walled valley carved
out by a river

clues (KLOOZ)
helpful hints that make it
easier for a person to solve a
mystery

descendants (di-SEND-uhnts)
living things that are related
to other living things from the
past

dynamite (DYE-nuh-mite)
a powerful explosive that is
used to blow things up

field notes (FEELD NOHTS)
information that a scientist
writes down while working and
exploring outside

fierce (FIHRSS)
very dangerous and violent

fossil field (FOSS-uhl FEELD)
a place where fossils are buried
in rocks

fossils (FOSS-uhlz)
what is left of plants or
animals that lived long ago

packs (PAKS)
groups

paleontologists
(*pale*-ee-uhn-TOL-uh-jists)
scientists who learn about
ancient life by studying fossils

plow (PLOU)
a tool used to dig up the
ground, usually so that a
farmer can plant things

quicksand (KWIK-sand)
wet, loose sand that someone
can sink into

site (SITE)
place or location

species (SPEE-sheez)
groups that animals are divided
into, according to similar
characteristics; members of
the same species can have
offspring together

tyrannosaurids (ti-*ran*-uh-SOR-idz)
a family of dinosaurs that
included some of the largest
and fiercest meat-eaters,
such as *Albertosaurus*,
Daspletosaurus, and *T. rex*

Bibliography

Bird, Ronald T. *Bones for Barnum Brown: Adventures of a Dinosaur Hunter.* Fort Worth, TX: Texas Christian University Press (1985).

Brown, Barnum. *Cretaceous Eocene Correlation in New Mexico, Wyoming, Montana, Alberta.* Bulletin of the Geological Society of America, 25:355–380 (1914).

Carpenter, Kenneth, and Philip J. Currie, eds. *Dinosaur Systematics: Approaches and Perspectives.* New York: Cambridge University Press (1992).

Currie, Philip J. *On a Pack of Theropods from Argentina.* Dino Press 1:79–89.

Currie, Philip J., and Eva B. Koppelhus, eds. *Dinosaur Provincial Park: A Spectacular Ancient Ecosystem Revealed.* Bloomington, IN: Indiana University Press (2005).

Read More

Felber, Eric P., and Philip J. Currie. *A Moment in Time with Albertosaurus.* Alberta: Troodon Productions, Inc. (2001).

Hartzog, Brooke. *Tyrannosaurus rex and Barnum Brown.* New York: PowerKids Press (1999).

Keiran, Monique. *Albertosaurus: Death of a Predator.* Vancouver: Raincoast Books (1999).

Spinar, Zdenek V., and Philip J. Currie. *Great Dinosaurs: From Triassic Through Jurassic to Cretaceous.* Stamford, CT: Longmeadow Press (1994).

Learn More Online

Visit these Web sites to learn more about Philip Currie, Barnum Brown, and *Albertosaurus*:

www.enchantedlearning.com/subjects/dinosaurs/dinos/Albertosaurus.shtml

www.fieldmuseum.org/exhibits/exhibit_sites/dino/Albertosaurus1.htm

www.nationalgeographic.com/ngkids/0005/dino/index.html

Index

About the Author

T. V. Padma is a writer and a scientist. She has written many books and articles for children, young adults, and adults. She also works at the University of Rhode Island's Graduate School.